THE TECH BEHIND
SELF-DRIVING CARS

by Matt Chandler

CAPSTONE PRESS
a capstone imprint

Edge Books are published by Capstone Press,
1710 Roe Crest Drive, North Mankato, Minnesota 56003
www.capstonepub.com

Copyright © 2020 by Capstone Press, a Capstone imprint. All rights reserved. No part of this publication may be reproduced in whole or in part, or stored in a retrieval system, or transmitted in any form or by any means, electronic, mechanical, photocopying, recording, or otherwise, without written permission of the publisher.

Library of Congress Cataloging-in-Publication Data
Names: Chandler, Matt, author.
Title: The tech behind self-driving cars / by Matt Chandler.
Description: North Mankato, Minnesota : Capstone Press,
  [2020] | Series: Edge books. Tech on wheels | Audience: Age 8-14. |
  Audience: Grade 4 to 6. | Includes bibliographical references and index.
Identifiers: LCCN 2018056094|
ISBN 9781543573053 (hardcover) | ISBN 9781543573091 (ebook pdf)
Subjects: LCSH: Autonomous vehicles—Juvenile literature. | Automobiles—Automatic control—Juvenile literature.
Classification: LCC TL152.8 .C45 2020 | DDC 629.222—dc23
LC record available at https://lccn.loc.gov/2018056094

Editorial Credits
Carrie Braulick Sheely, editor; Jennifer Bergstrom, designer; Eric Gohl, media researcher; Katy LaVigne, production specialist

Photo Credits
Alamy: fStop Images GmbH, 28; Getty Images: Bettmann, 7; Newscom: Reuters/Aaron Josefczyk, 12, Reuters/Elijah Nouvelage, 4, Reuters/Natalie Behring, 10, Reuters/Rebecca Cook, 24, Sipa USA/Kris Tripplaar, 23; Shutterstock: Flystock, 8, 20, Loralya, 19, metamorworks, 18, 26, posteriori, 22, Scharfsinn, 14, Sean Leonard, cover, temp-64GTX, 16

Design Elements: Shutterstock

All internet sites appearing in back matter were available and accurate when this book was sent to press.

Printed in and bound in the USA.
PA70

TABLE OF CONTENTS

CHAPTER 1
Spotlight on Self-Driving Cars 4

CHAPTER 2
Cutting-Edge Tech 8

CHAPTER 3
Putting the Data to Work 16

CHAPTER 4
Focus on Safety 20

CHAPTER 5
Driving into the Future 24

Glossary 30
Read More 31
Internet Sites 31
Index 32

A self-driving Chevy Bolt drives during a media event in San Francisco, California, in 2017.

CHAPTER 1

SPOTLIGHT ON SELF-DRIVING CARS

Imagine cruising down the highway in your parents' car. You look out the window and see a car passing. A boy and girl about your age are in the back seat. A grown-up is in the passenger seat. But the driver's seat is empty! How is that possible?

Fully self-driving cars aren't yet available for the public to buy. But car manufacturers have been developing and testing autonomous cars for almost 100 years. They use many types of advanced technology to replace human drivers. It might seem impossible now, but experts believe self-driving cars will be common on the roads someday.

Would you feel safe in a car with no driver? Manufacturers are packing these cars with amazing technology to make them as safe as possible. Certain self-driving features are already in some cars. With each new part or design idea, fully self-driving cars take a step closer to reality.

autonomous—able to operate without outside control

History of Self-driving Cars

The history of self-driving cars goes back to the early 1900s. In 1925, crowds lined Broadway in New York City one summer afternoon to watch history be made. Army veteran Francis Houdina was about to test the first driverless car on a city street. Houdina modified a 1926 Chandler sedan to make it run without a driver. The technology wasn't very advanced compared to today. Houdina attached an antenna to the top of the Chandler. Another car drove behind it. The second vehicle sent signals to the antenna. These signals went to small engines fitted inside the Chandler. The signals told the engine to speed up, change direction, or brake. A signal could even honk the car's horn.

FACT Houdina knew his driverless car might have problems. The inventor rode on the running board of the car during the test. He planned to grab the wheel and take over if there was an emergency.

modify—to change in some way

Houdina's car traveled smoothly through rush-hour traffic for a short time. But then it crashed into the back of another vehicle, ending the historic test. Even though his car crashed, Houdina had proven a car could operate without a driver behind the wheel. His test led others to build their own versions of self-driving cars.

Houdina's self-driving car (front) drove through busy streets in New York City in 1925.

A man lets go of the steering wheel of a Tesla Model S to allow it to drive by itself.

CHAPTER 2

CUTTING-EDGE TECH

Self-driving technology has come a long way from the early 1900s. Today car manufacturers invest millions of dollars in self-driving technology. These companies include Google, Tesla, Nissan, Ford, and Uber.

Even though fully self-driving cars are not legal on the roads, plenty of self-driving technology is in use. One is parking assistance. A car with this feature has sensors and cameras that act as the eyes of the driver. In some systems, if the car gets too close to an object, the system will warn the driver. In other systems, the parking assist feature controls the steering too. Some Tesla Model S cars can even park themselves in a garage without the driver!

LEVELS OF SELF-DRIVING CARS

The Society of Automotive Engineers created levels of self-driving vehicles.

Level 0: No self-driving features are used.

Level 1: Driver Assistance—The car may have one or more systems that can control speed or steering, but not both at the same time. Automatic emergency braking is an example of a Level 1 feature.

Level 2: Partial Automation—The car has combined self-driving features with the ability to control both steering and speed at the same time. The driver must still be tracking the car's surroundings and be ready to take control.

Level 3: Conditional Automation—The car has Level 2 features and it can monitor the surroundings. The system can notify the driver to take action if there is a situation it can't handle. The driver must be available to take over at all times.

Level 4: High Automation—The car can operate by itself, but only under certain conditions. Road type, location, or other conditions could require the driver to take over.

Level 5: Full Automation—The car can operate by itself under all conditions.

sensor—an instrument that detects changes and sends information to a controlling device

How Self-Driving Cars See

If you try to walk with your eyes closed, you will probably bump into a lot of things. Self-driving cars need to see where they are going too.

Radar is often located in the front bumper of a self-driving car. It scans several feet in front of the car. The radar detects objects and their distance from the car. If the object is moving, radar can find its speed.

The lidar spins on top of a self-driving car's roof.

Some car manufacturers, such as Waymo, use lidar instead of radar. Lidar is a roof-mounted device that rotates. It captures 360-degree views of a car's surroundings. The lidar device continually spins while sending out beams of light. These beams bounce off objects, including lane markers, stop signs, and other cars. Lidar is more accurate than radar. It can also detect more details.

FACT
Lidar sends out up to 150,000 pulses per second.

radar—an electronic device that uses radio waves to determine the location of an object

Self-driving cars can have as many as 12 video cameras. These high-resolution cameras see detail well. They also work at very high speeds. The faster they work, the faster the car can react to a change. Cameras do not work as well in low light. Weather conditions such as snow or rain can also affect them. For this reason, self-driving car manufacturers usually combine them with radar or lidar.

The video cameras on a self-driving car are often built into other parts, such as mirrors.

Technology That Blends In

Were you expecting that self-driving car that just passed you to look more like a spaceship? If so, you might have been disappointed.

Most of the self-driving technology in today's cars is barely noticeable. Sensors and cameras are built into the bumpers or sides of the car so they blend in. A car's body design is a big reason why people choose to buy a certain car. Developers of self-driving cars want the vehicles to still be attractive to buyers. After all, no one wants an ugly car! Tesla CEO Elon Musk took an extra step to avoid visible sensors on the outside of the company's Model X. Tesla invented a sensor that can send sonar waves through metal. The sensors are inside the doors.

resolution—a measure of the sharpness of an image

sonar—a device that measures the distance to an object by bouncing sound waves off the object and timing how long it takes the waves to return

Map It!

Have you ever needed a map to know where to go? Self-driving cars use maps too. They take information gathered from the cameras and lidar to create an internal map. A Tesla Model 3 has eight cameras mounted around the car. The cameras can "see" objects up to 820 feet (250 meters) away. The computer in the car creates a three-dimensional (3-D) map from the images collected. This internal map works with a global positioning system (GPS) to help the car navigate.

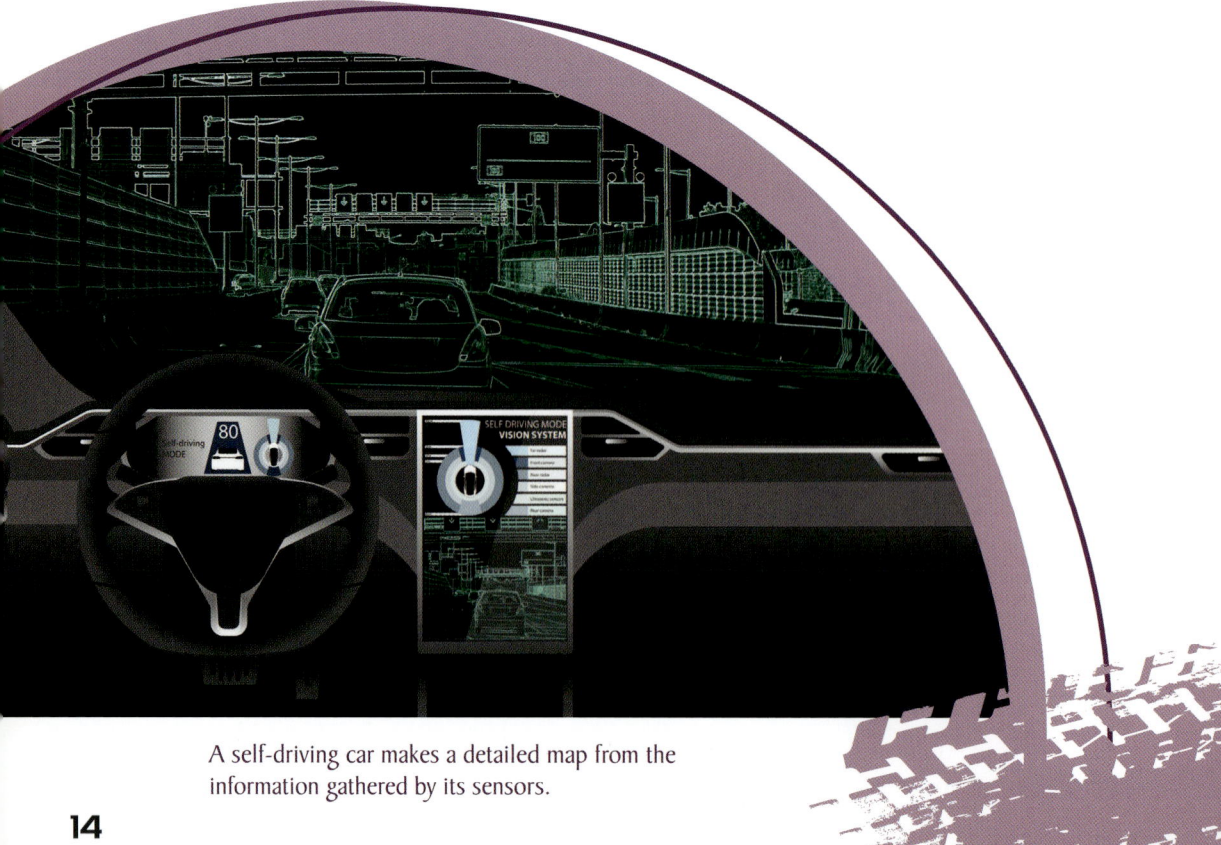

A self-driving car makes a detailed map from the information gathered by its sensors.

Super-Smart Software

How is it possible to re-create the brain and actions of a human driver? All the data gathered by the cameras, sensors, and mapping system in a self-driving car feeds into a computer. This computer uses software to organize the information and make decisions. Artificial intelligence (AI) software makes the car smarter. The software gathers data and images every time the car is driven. This information is mapped and stored for later use. For example, once a car has driven on a certain road, it can remember the location of the curves and the stop signs.

artificial intelligence—the ability of a machine to learn

global positioning system—a system that receives signals from satellites in the sky to find the location of objects

software—the programs that tell the hardware of the computer what to do

15

An actuator would apply the emergency brakes if a self-driving car sensed that the car in front of it suddenly slowed down.

CHAPTER 3

PUTTING THE DATA TO WORK

After the computer decides what to do, it's time for parts in the car to get moving. This is where actuators come into play. If the sensors and cameras on the car are the eyes and ears of a driver, the actuator is the muscle in charge of taking action.

Imagine a sensor identifies a road sign that shows the speed limit is increasing. This data goes to the computer. The computer recognizes the need to speed up. It signals the actuator, which is programmed to respond. The actuator presses down the gas pedal to increase speed. An actuator would also go to work if the car needed to apply the brakes or control the steering.

An actuator might also get the message not to take action. Imagine a car is at a stop sign. The traffic light turns green. But there is an object in the car's way. The actuator would then get the message to keep applying the brakes.

FACT
Today many cars come with a self-driving feature called adaptive cruise control. This feature uses cameras and sensors to monitor traffic. If the car in front speeds up or slows down, the computer sends a signal to the actuator to do the same.

actuator—a mechanical device for moving or controlling something

Putting It All Together

Picture a car zipping down the road. Suddenly, a large box falls off a truck in front of the car. The driver makes a split-second decision and swerves. A self-driving car's computer would need to do the same thing.

A self-driving car's sensors are constantly keeping track of what is happening around it. This monitoring allows it to act quickly to avoid an accident.

In this situation, the car's sensors and cameras would see the box. They would signal the central computer that there is a problem. The computer would access the data it had stored. This information could include a map of the road. It may also include information on how it avoided a similar object in the past. The computer would use the information to find the safest way to avoid an accident. It would send a signal to the actuator to take action. A potential accident could be avoided thanks to amazing technology.

FACT

In Australia, Volvo's self-driving tech was tripped up by kangaroos! Because kangaroos hop, the car's sensors reported different distances to the animals. Volvo is working to fix the problem before it launches its self-driving cars.

The IMU always knows the car's exact position on the road.

CHAPTER 4

FOCUS ON SAFETY

Safety is a priority for most car buyers. This will be especially true for those considering buying fully self-driving cars in the future. The tech in these cars will keep the passengers as safe as possible.

Inertial Measurement Unit

GPS is important to the operation of a self-driving car. But GPS relies on satellite signals to operate. If a self-driving car was using only GPS and the signal was lost, it could crash. As a backup system to GPS, a self-driving car has an Inertial Measurement Unit (IMU).

Anytime the car is running, the IMU monitors all the sensors on the vehicle. This ability allows it to always know the vehicle's position on the road. Imagine there is a sharp curve in the road ahead and the GPS signal is lost. The IMU unit would step in and analyze the information from the sensors. The IMU signals the actuator to turn the wheel or apply the brakes to adjust for the curve ahead. The IMU is incredibly accurate. It can maintain steering accuracy to within 12 inches (30 centimeters).

Smart Object Discrimination Tech

What is that object up ahead? Is it a person, a rolling ball, or something else? People can quickly identify objects. Self-driving cars need to have fast object discrimination too. Waymo uses a unique technology to help its cars identify people. Software designers upload thousands of images of people for the car's computer to analyze. The images include people walking, jogging, and crossing streets. The software "memorizes" all the images. When lidar detects an object in the road, the car will compare it with its memory bank of images. It can then identify if it is a person.

Self-driving cars must quickly and accurately identify objects.

WHEN TECHNOLOGY FAILS

In 2018, a fully self-driving Uber test car struck and killed a pedestrian in Tempe, Arizona. The car's sensors recognized her, but the car's emergency braking system had been disabled. The person in the car also failed to take over and apply the brakes. Uber stopped testing its self-driving cars for nine months and took action to make its cars and testing process safer.

Uber has tested many self-driving vehicles in Arizona.

Waymo also uses machine learning to build models that predict peoples' movements. Sometimes people will walk halfway across a busy street and pause in the middle for traffic to clear on the other side. Waymo has made a model where its cars will recognize that as unusual behavior and slow down. The models prepare the car for pedestrians not using crosswalks or crossing at a green light. These models of human behavior are stored in the software. The cars are then better prepared for unexpected situations.

23

Ford displayed a self-driving Fusion at the North American International Auto Show in 2018.

CHAPTER 5

DRIVING INTO THE FUTURE

With the money car manufacturers are investing, the tech in self-driving cars is getting more advanced. But there are still plenty of challenges to overcome before fully self-driving cars fill the streets.

Costly Tech

If the fully self-driving cars being tested today were suddenly made available for purchase, many people couldn't afford them. Experts say the cost to make a car fully autonomous adds at least $8,000 to the bill. If self-driving cars are going to be a reality in the future, reducing the cost will be important.

Ford is among those leading the way. The company says it will have a fleet of fully self-driving vehicles for sale by 2021. Ford plans to avoid costly extras, such as a feature that directs a car to pick up people from their locations. Ford says its cars will be affordable for the general public.

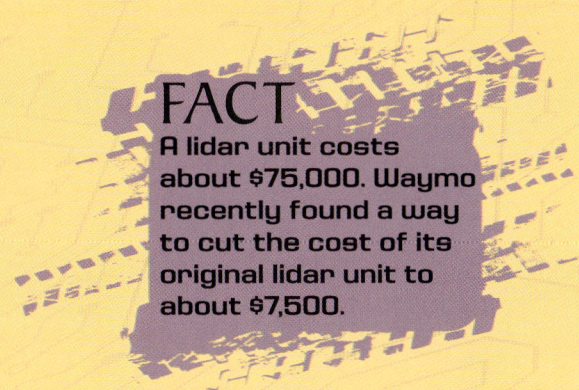

FACT
A lidar unit costs about $75,000. Waymo recently found a way to cut the cost of its original lidar unit to about $7,500.

Car Conversations

As your dad pulls up to an intersection, he extends his hand out the window to motion another car to go first. He explains to you that the turn signal on the car is broken. He needed a way to communicate with the other driver to help avoid an accident. Engineers believe self-driving cars will be able to communicate with one another in a similar way to help avoid crashes.

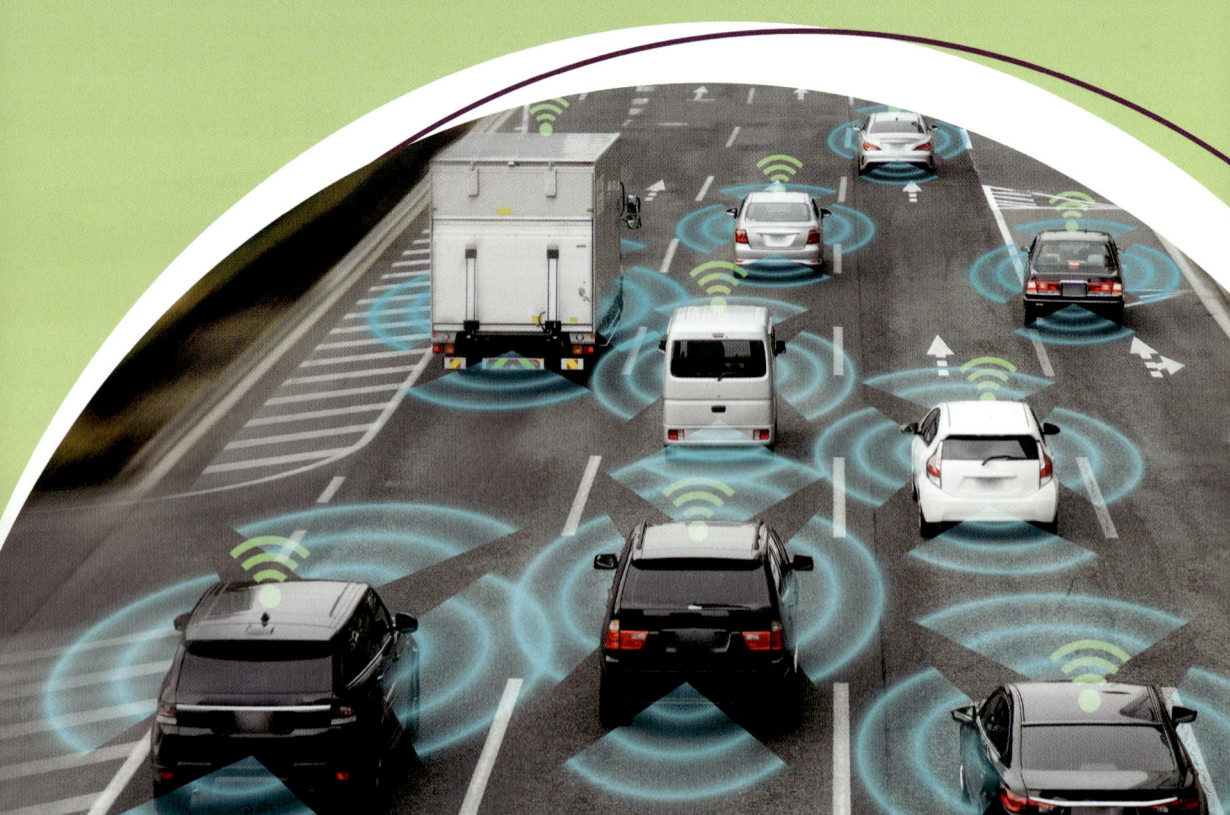

V2V technology would allow self-driving cars to communicate messages to one another.

Vehicle to vehicle (V2V) is a technology that can allow this communication to happen. It will use wireless technology known as Dedicated Short Range Communication. V2V will allow a car to send as many as 10 messages per second. The messages will be able to communicate information about another vehicle's speed, position, and direction. Imagine you are in a car heading toward an intersection. A car approaching from another direction isn't stopping. Your car could receive a message from the other vehicle and automatically apply the brakes to avoid a crash.

Developers say V2V tech isn't limited just to cars. With the technology in place, cars might also be able to communicate directly to traffic lights.

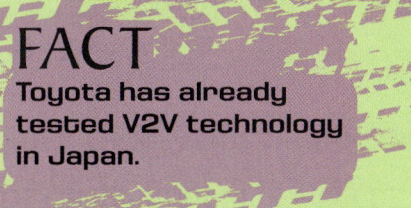

FACT
Toyota has already tested V2V technology in Japan.

Lighting the Way with Lasers

What if cars could see objects not only in front of them and around them, but also around a corner? Researchers at Stanford University are working to make that a reality. They have developed a system for non-line-of-sight imaging. They think the system could work when a laser is directed at an angle toward an object. The light bounces off the object and goes around a corner. The light then hits the object around the corner and bounces back to a scanner on the car. The car's computer will collect the data and make an image of the object that is out of sight. The computer will send a signal to the actuator to react.

Scientists have tested lasers to detect unmoving objects around a corner. Further testing will help the lasers detect objects in motion, such as bouncing balls.

One Piece of Technology at a Time

Experts are not sure when fully self-driving cars might be part of everyday life. In the meantime, car manufacturers continue to add self-driving technology to existing cars. Each one brings us a step closer to a day when driving a car may be a thing of the past.

DATA DANGERS

A group of scientists in China were able to jam the system of a self-driving car using standard radio equipment. The signal from the hackers' car blocked the radio waves sent from a Tesla so it could not recognize that there was an object in front of it. If this were a real-life situation, the results could have been deadly. Manufacturers continue to develop technology to protect their systems from being hacked. In 2016, Fiat Chrysler partnered with hackers. The automaker offered $1,500 to hackers who could find a weak spot in the software that would make it easy to hack.

hacker—a person who looks for ways to break into computer systems

GLOSSARY

actuator (AK-chuh-way-tur)—a mechanical device for moving or controlling something

artificial intelligence (ar-ti-FISH-uhl in-TEL-uh-jens)—the ability of a machine to learn

autonomous (AWE-tah-nuh-muhs)—able to operate without outside control

global positioning system (GLOH-buhl puh-ZI-shuh-ning SISS-tuhm)—a system that receives signals from satellites in the sky to find the location of an object

hacker (HAK-ur)—a person who looks for ways to break into computer systems

modify (MAH-duh-fye)—to change in some way

radar (RAY-dar)—an electronic device that uses radio waves to determine the location of an object

resolution (re-zuh-LOO-shuhn)—a measure of the sharpness of an image

sensor (SEN-sur)—an instrument that detects changes and sends information to a controlling device

software (SAWFT-wair)—the programs that tell the hardware of the computer what to do

sonar (SOH-nar)—a device that measures the distance to an object by bouncing sound waves off the object and timing how long it takes the waves to return

READ MORE

Bethea, Nikole Brooks. *High-Tech Highways and Super Skyways: The Next 100 Years of Transportation.* Our World: The Next 100 Years. North Mankato, MN: Capstone Press, 2017.

Enz, Tammy. *Artificial Intelligence at Home and on the Go: 4D An Augmented Reading Experience.* The World of Artificial Intelligence 4D. North Mankato, MN: Capstone, 2019.

Gitlin, Marty. *Careers in Self-Driving Car Technology.* Emerging Tech Careers. North Mankato, MN: Cherry Lake Pub., 2019.

INTERNET SITES

Guide to Self-Driving Cars
https://www.consumerreports.org/autonomous-driving/self-driving-cars-guide/

Here's How the Sensors in Autonomous Cars Work
http://www.thedrive.com/tech/8657/heres-how-the-sensors-in-autonomous-cars-work

What Are the Different Self-Driving Car "Levels" of Autonomy?
https://www.howtogeek.com/401759/what-are-the-different-self-driving-car-levels-of-autonomy/

INDEX

actuators, 16, 17, 19, 21, 28
artificial intelligence (AI), 15
autonomous, 5, 25

cameras, 9, 12, 13, 14, 15, 16, 17, 19
crashes, 7, 21, 26, 27

Dedicated Short Range Communication, 27

engineers, 26

Ford, 8, 25

global positioning system (GPS), 14, 21
Google, 8

hackers, 29
Houdina, Francis, 6, 7

Inertial Measurement Unit (IMU), 21

lasers, 28
lidar, 11, 12, 14, 22, 25

maps, 14, 15, 19
Musk, Elon, 13

New York City, 6
Nissan, 8

object discrimination, 22

pedestrians, 23

radar, 10, 11, 12
radio waves, 29
resolution, 12

sensors, 9, 13, 15, 16, 17, 19, 21, 23
software, 15, 22, 23, 29
sonar, 13
Stanford University, 28

Tesla, 8, 9, 13, 14, 29

Uber, 8, 23

vehicle to vehicle (V2V), 27

Waymo, 11, 22, 23, 25